Numeracy Focus

Class Focus Book 5

Written and edited by
Sheila Ebbutt and Mike Askew

with contributions from Len Frobisher, Kate Frood,
Jeremy Hodgen and John Spooner

RIGBY

Place value grid

100 000	200 000	300 000	400 000	500 000
10 000	20 000	30 000	40 000	50 000
1000	2000	3000	4000	5000
100	200	300	400	500
10	20	30	40	50
1	2	3	4	5
0·1	0·2	0·3	0·4	0·5
0·01	0·02	0·03	0·04	0·05

600 000	700 000	800 000	900 000
60 000	70 000	80 000	90 000
6000	7000	8000	9000
600	700	800	900
60	70	80	90
6	7	8	9
0·6	0·7	0·8	0·9
0·06	0·07	0·08	0·09

10 × 10 multiplication grid

✕	1	2	3	4	5	6	7	8	9	10
1	1	2	3	4	5	6	7	8	9	10
2	2	4	6	8	10	12	14	16	18	20
3	3	6	9	12	15	18	21	24	27	30
4	4	8	12	16	20	24	28	32	36	40
5	5	10	15	20	25	30	35	40	45	50
6	6	12	18	24	30	36	42	48	54	60
7	7	14	21	28	35	42	49	56	63	70
8	8	16	24	32	40	48	56	64	72	80
9	9	18	27	36	45	54	63	72	81	90
10	10	20	30	40	50	60	70	80	90	100

1	2	3	4	5	6	7	8	9	10
11	12	13	14	15	16	17	18	19	20
21	22	23	24	25	26	27	28	29	30
31	32	33	34	35	36	37	38	39	40
41	42	43	44	45	46	47	48	49	50
51	52	53	54	55	56	57	58	59	60
61	62	63	64	65	66	67	68	69	70
71	72	73	74	75	76	77	78	79	80
81	82	83	84	85	86	87	88	89	90
91	92	93	94	95	96	97	98	99	100

1a

1 fifty-two thousand three hundred and forty-seven

2 eight hundred and twenty thousand four hundred and sixty-seven

3 six hundred and seventy-two thousand and thirteen

4 nine hundred and three thousand two hundred and fifty-four

1b

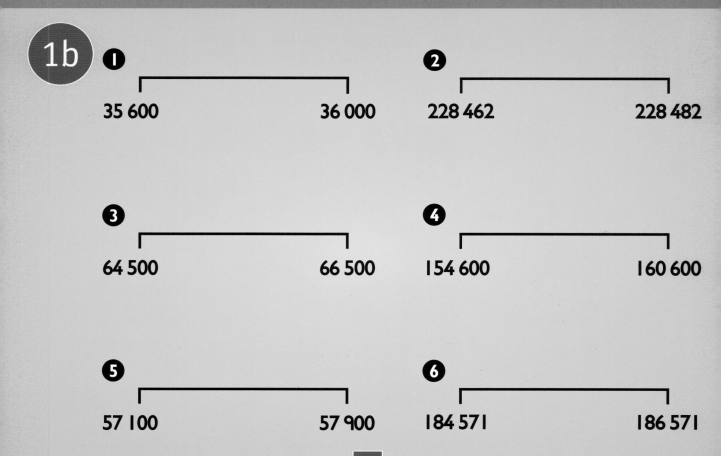

1

35 600   36 000

2

228 462   228 482

3

64 500   66 500

4

154 600   160 600

5

57 100   57 900

6

184 571   186 571

999

5432　　　　4090

x10

6392　　　　8020

x100

1001　　　7093

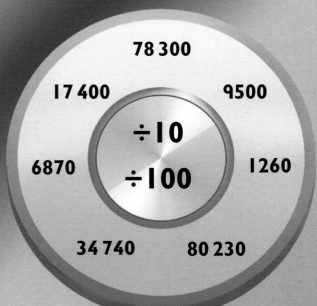

78 300

17 400　　　　9500

÷10

6870　　　　1260

÷100

34 740　　　80 230

2a **A** **❶** | 230 ⟵ 460 ⟶ 920

❷ | ? ⟵ 380 ⟶ ?

❸ | ? ⟵ 230 ⟶ ?

❹ | ? ⟵ 840 ⟶ ?

❺ | ? ⟵ 390 ⟶ ?

❻ | ? ⟵ 136 ⟶ ?

❼ | ? ⟵ 670 ⟶ ?

2	3	5	7	9
8	10	16	28	4
112	72	6	48	12
18	80	36	40	32
56		24	20	14

2b

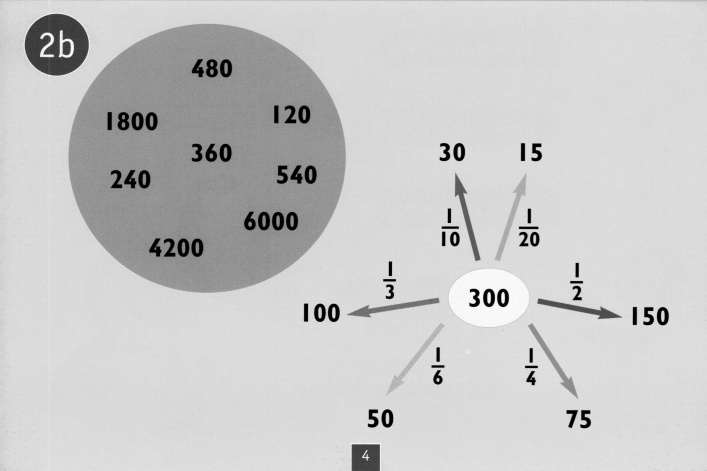

480

1800

120

360

240

540

6000

4200

30   15

$\frac{1}{10}$ $\frac{1}{20}$

$\frac{1}{3}$ $\frac{1}{2}$

100   **300**   150

$\frac{1}{6}$ $\frac{1}{4}$

50   75

3a

1. 347 x 8
2. 342 x 3
3. 212 x 4
4. 603 x 5
5. 491 x 3
6. 322 x 8
7. 281 x 5
8. 172 x 9
9. 709 x 6
10. 559 x 7
11. 779 x 6
12. 537 x 5

3b

1. 4.6 x 6
2. 7.4 x 4
3. 1.9 x 7
4. 2.6 x 3
5. 6.7 x 5
6. 8.6 x 8
7. 5.7 x 4
8. 3.9 x 9
9. 2.7 x 7
10. 11.7 x 8

3c

1

Kids' corner
£2.85

7 friends go

2

Swimming pool
£2.40

8 children go

3

Pizza £3.55

6 friends eat

4

BOWLING

Bowling £1.27

4 children go

5

ZOO
£4·49

The zoo £4.49

5 friends go

6

Ice skating £3.79

6 friends go

A **1**

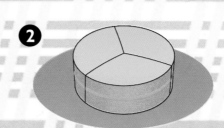

$3\frac{1}{2}$ whole cakes

7 halves of a whole cake

3

4

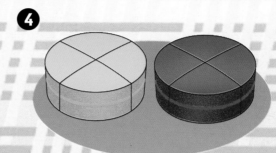

5

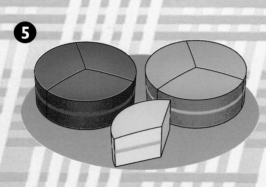

6

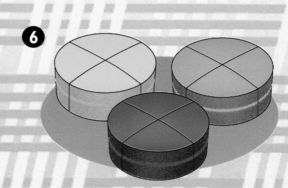

B **1**

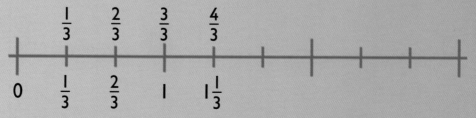

2

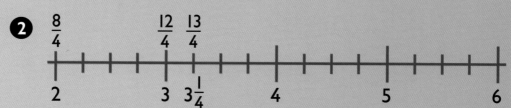

10 906 pennies

6999 pennies

450 170 pennies

1004 pennies

147 pennies

£108.42

£25.00

£0.96

£4.99

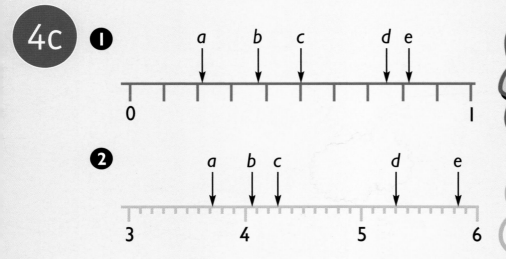

1

0   *a*   *b*   *c*   *d* *e*   1

0·6   0·5
2·1   0·21
0·75   0·38
3·8   8·2
0·82

2

3   *a*   *b* *c*   4   *d*   5   *e*   6

53   5·3
37·2   6·4
4·06   5·83
7·32   46
3·72   4·29

①

Strawberry Jam 400g

20 g of fruit in every 100 g

60 g of sugar in every 100 g

②

Blackberry 300g

20 g of fruit in every 100 g

40 g of sugar in every 100 g

③

Marmalade 20g

1 g of fruit in every 5 g

3 g of sugar in every 10 g

④

Gooseberry Jam 500g

3 g of fruit in every 10 g

8 g of sugar in every 20 g

⑤

RASPBERRY 600g

15 g of fruit in every 100 g

70 g of sugar in every 100 g

①

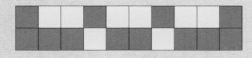

②

③

④

⑤

⑥

⑦

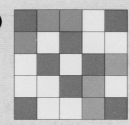

A

1. 632 + 464
2. 562 − 146
3. 62 × 6
4. 206 − 63
5. 26 + 146
6. 616 − 263
7. 36 × 16
8. 666 − 86

B

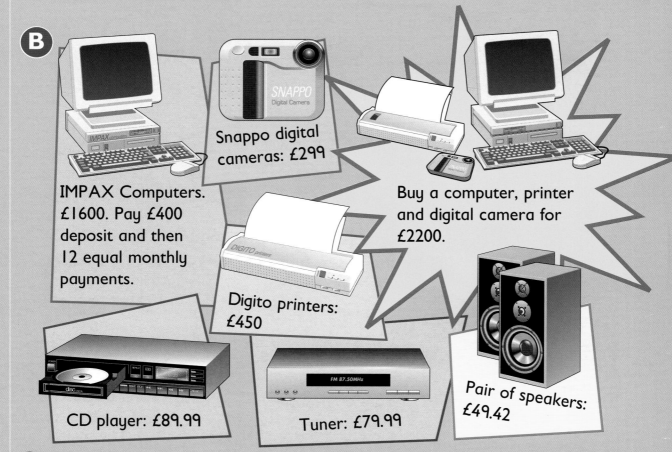

IMPAX Computers. £1600. Pay £400 deposit and then 12 equal monthly payments.

Snappo digital cameras: £299

Buy a computer, printer and digital camera for £2200.

Digito printers: £450

CD player: £89.99

Tuner: £79.99

Pair of speakers: £49.42

1. How much can you save by buying a computer, printer and digital camera as a set rather than separately?

2. Mrs Pental is buying a computer. How much will she have to pay each month?

3. Josie is saving up for a digital camera. She started with £50 and saved £12.50 each month for a year. How much longer does she have to save for?

4. Sameer has got £250 for a hi-fi. If he buys a CD player, tuner and pair of speakers, how much will he have left for buying CDs?

Write the numbers of children for each column of these two graphs.

1

Beech school's favourite areas of Elm Park, by Yellow Class

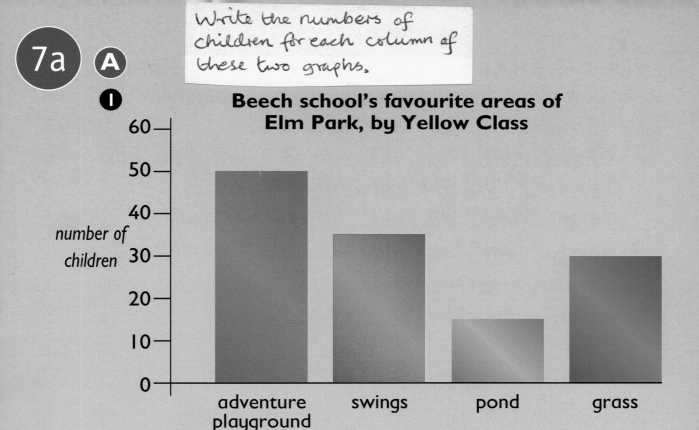

2

Numbers of children using Elm Park facilities on Sunday 14 July (information from Local Council)

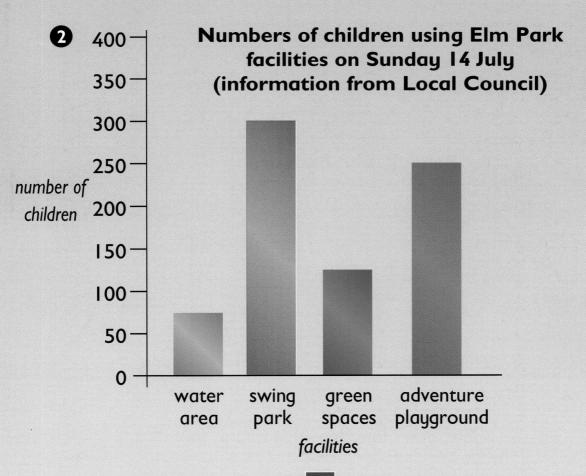

Yellow class did a survey of children at the school on 5 July.
'On how many days did you use Elm Park last week?'

0 days	ⵌ ⵌ ⵌ ⵌ //
1-2 days	ⵌ ⵌ ⵌ ⵌ ⵌ ⵌ ⵌ ⵌ
3-4 days	ⵌ ⵌ ⵌ ⵌ ⵌ ⵌ
5-6 days	ⵌ ⵌ ⵌ ⵌ ⵌ ⵌ ///
7 days	ⵌ ⵌ ⵌ ⵌ ⵌ ⵌ ⵌ /

7b Children using Elm Park, 25 – 31 January.

Day	Time				
	9 a.m. to noon	noon to 3 p.m.	3 p.m. to 6 p.m.	6 p.m. to 9 p.m.	9 p.m. to midnight
Mon	1	0	0	0	0
Tues	0	3	4	3	0
Wed	2	0	0	0	0
Thurs	0	5	12	2	0
Fri	3	2	20	2	0
Sat	54	35	67	0	0
Sun	0	0	0	0	0

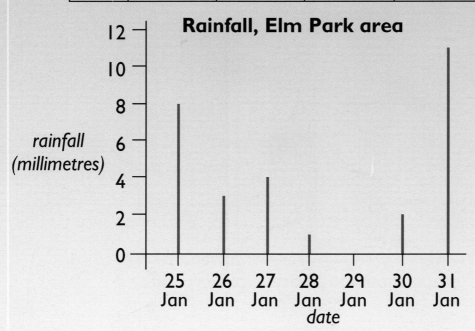

Rainfall, Elm Park area

rainfall (millimetres)

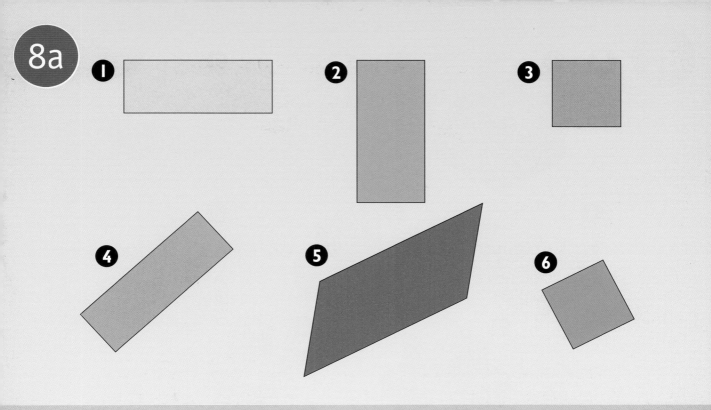

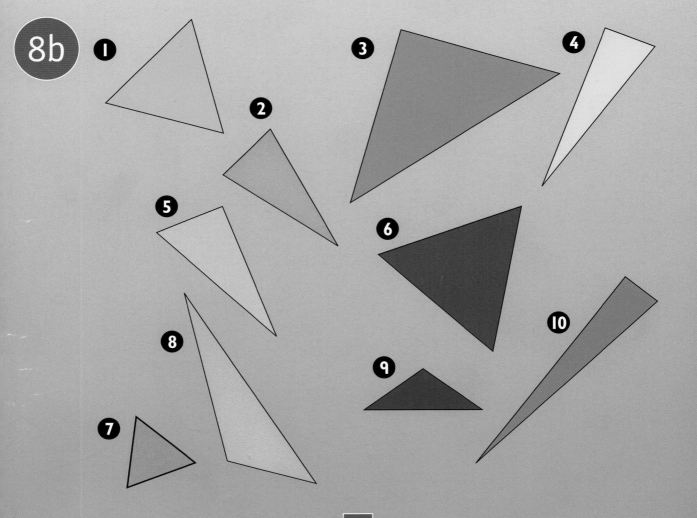

A

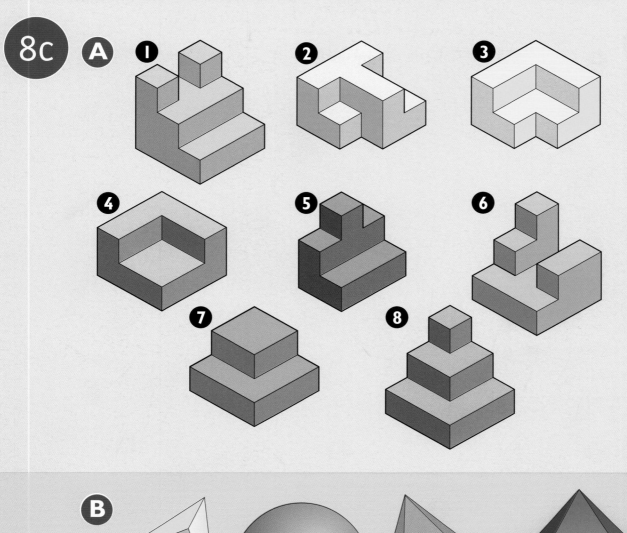

B

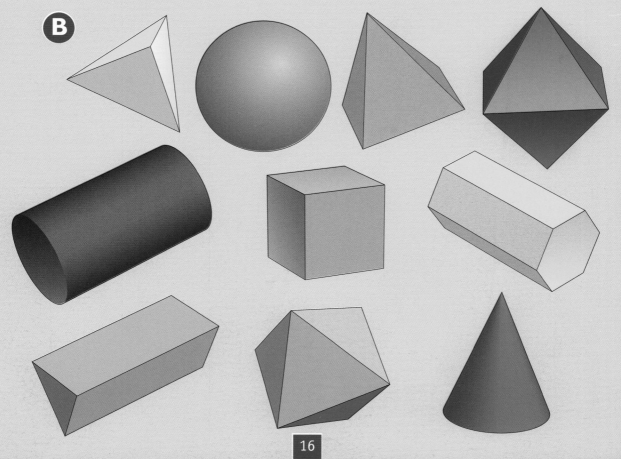

A

35 mm

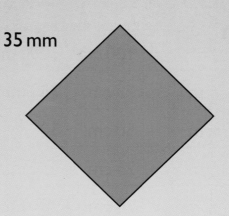

Each side is 35 mm

4 times 35 is 140

The perimeter is 140 mm

1

2

3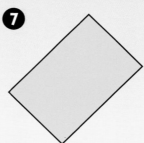

4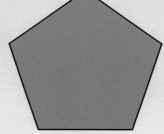

5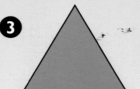

6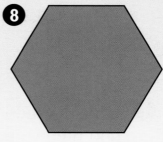

7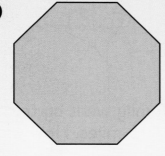

8

B

shape	perimeter	length of each side
equilateral triangle	600 mm	
square	600 mm	
regular pentagon	600 mm	
regular hexagon	600 mm	

A

1 m	100 cm	1000 mm	1·0 m
$\frac{3}{4}$ m	75 cm	750 mm	0·75 m
$\frac{1}{2}$ m	50 cm	500 mm	0·5 m
$\frac{1}{4}$ m	25 cm	250 mm	0·25 m
$\frac{1}{10}$ m	10 cm	100 mm	0·1 m
$\frac{1}{100}$ m	1 cm	10 mm	0·01 m

B

1 Little Tweedon is 150 miles away. The family went by train and then by bus. The train journey was 115 miles. How many miles did they travel by bus?

2 The tallest building in Little Tweedon village is half a metre high. The smallest is 25 cm. What is the difference in their heights?

3 In Millennium Lane they have built new houses. The plot for each house is 50 cm wide. Millennium Lane is 6 metres long. How many houses did they build?

4 Each little window pane in the village shop is 10 mm high. The window is 4 panes high. What is the height of the window in centimetres?

5 The barn door is 5 cm wide. The model cow is 10 mm narrower than the door. How wide is the model cow?

 **1** My film starts at quarter past seven this evening, and lasts for one hour fifty minutes.

 **2** My favourite after-school TV programme is from four thirty-five until ten past five.

3 I'm going to karate from six until seven-thirty this evening.

I go to play-centre after school from three-thirty until six. **4**

 **5** My Saturday morning Drama School starts at ten and lasts for two and a half hours.

6 My bus leaves at ten past ten this morning and I arrive in Leeds at quarter past eleven.

The match starts at quarter to eight this evening and ends at nine-thirty. **7**

My Dad works nightshifts from ten, until seven in the morning. **8**

10b **A**

Date	Sunrise	Sunset	Date	Sunrise	Sunset	Date	Sunrise	Sunset
I Jan	08:05	16:05	I May	05:30	20:35	I Sept	06:10	19:50
I Feb	07:40	16:55	I June	04:55	21:15	I Oct	07:00	18:22
I Mar	06:50	17:48	I July	04:58	21:20	I Nov	07:10	16:30
I Apr	06:27	19:45	I Aug	05:30	20:48	I Dec	07:45	15:55

B Train timetable

leaves Broxham	09:20	09:50	and at these times past each hour until 21:50	leaves Caverley Zoo	12:45	13:15	and at these times past each hour until 22:15
arrives Caverley Zoo	10:40	11:10		arrives Broxham	14:05	14:35	

Caverley Zoo

Open from 09:30 until sunset

Meet the elephants (30 minutes)

09:30	15:30
10:30	16:30
11:30	

Boat rides on the river through the aviary (90 minutes)

11:15
13:15
15:15
17:15

Camel rides (20 minutes)

Every half hour from 10:30 until 16:00

Have your photograph taken with a bird of prey!

Photos ready one hour later

Open 09:30 – 16:00

Café open from 09:30 to 15 minutes before closing

From 12:00 until 14:00
Minimum charge per head is £3

Endangered species – how you can help

Film show and talk – 40 minutes

12:00
16:00

Penguin feeding times (15 minutes)

12:30   16:30

11a

1
462	514
625	971
874	703

2
189	395
176	267
286	308

11b

1

Sanjay scored 356 on level 1 and 268 on level 2. What is his total score?

2

Emma scored 604 and Grace scored 476. How much more did Emma score than Grace?

3

Victoria and Michael are working as a team. Victoria has scored 787 and Michael has scored 559. How much they have altogether?

4

Ed has to score 458 to catch up with Victoria and Michael. What is Ed's score?

1 ✧ ✧ ✧   12   18   24   30   ✧ ✧ ✧

2 ✴ ✴ ✴   11   19   27   35   ✴ ✴ ✴

3 ❂ ❂ ❂   43   34   25   16   ❂ ❂ ❂

4 ♣ ♣ ♣   0·7   1·4   2·1   2·8   ♣ ♣ ♣

5 ❀ ❀ ❀   15   30   45   60   ❀ ❀ ❀

6 ⍟ ⍟ ⍟   29   22   15   8   ⍟ ⍟ ⍟

7 ★ ★ ★   22   33   44   55   ★ ★ ★

8 ☆ ☆ ☆   −22   −16   −10   −4   ☆ ☆ ☆

9 ✳ ✳ ✳   2·8   2·6   2·4   2·2   ✳ ✳ ✳

10 ❋ ❋ ❋   240   190   140   90   ❋ ❋ ❋

| True | False |

1 I found a square number that ends in 0.

2 I found a 2-digit square number with both digits even.

3 I found a square number that ends in 7.

4 I found a 2-digit square number with both digits odd.

5 I found a square number between 200 and 300.

12c

You can arrange 30 tiles to make exactly 4 different rectangles. What number of tiles makes exactly 5 different rectangles?

1

maximum 50 seats

2

No more than 14 people

3

To pass the test, you have to get more than 10 answers correct.

4

Sugar Plum Ballet School

To be a ballet dancer, you have to be at least 1·68 m tall.

5

Heavyweight division: 88 kg or more.

6

30

30 miles per hour maximum speed

7

Health information

If your body temperature goes over 37°C you should see the doctor.

8

Agitator Alligator Ride

Are you tall enough?

1·5 m minimum height

B

10569

10659

10695

91 065

91 056

901 065

100 695

56 901

65 109

91 605

59 106

95 601

50 961

56 196

51 996

56 109

56 190

65 911

13b

❶ 0, −3, −6, −9, −12, −15, −18

❷ 1, −3, −7, −11, −15, −19, −23

❸ 3, −3, −9, −15, −21, −27, −33

❹ 41, 34, 27, 20, 13, 6, −1

❺ 4, −1, __, −11, −16, __, −26

❻ __, 35, 27, __, 11, 3, __

14a **A**
1. 23 × 12
2. 12 × 31
3. 22 × 13
4. 15 × 14
5. 14 × 13

B
1. 42 × 21   42 × 19
2. 24 × 21   24 × 19
3. 16 × 21   16 × 19
4. 33 × 21   33 × 19
5. 51 × 21   51 × 19

14b
1. 22 × 6
2. 4 × 34
3. 68 × 3
4. 47 × 5
5. 6 × 73
6. 7 × 36
7. 63 × 8
8. 76 × 6

14c
1. 45 × 6 = ☁
2. ☁ ÷ 4 = 26
3. ☁ ÷ 37 = 5
4. 6 × ☁ = 90
5. ☁ × 3 = 69
6. ☁ × 6 = 72
7. ☁ ÷ 15 = 12
8. 32 × 21 = ☁
9. ☁ ÷ 19 = 23
10. 32 × 6 = ☁

28

15a

1. $613 \div 6$
2. $539 \div 4$
3. $346 \div 6$
4. $557 \div 8$
5. $709 \div 9$
6. $549 \div 5$

15b

A

$4\overline{)573}$

$3\overline{)226}$

$6\overline{)457}$

$7\overline{)419}$

$9\overline{)847}$

B

$4\overline{)573}$

$3\overline{)197}$

$4\overline{)338}$

$8\overline{)637}$

$7\overline{)646}$

15c

1. Ms Patel collects 258 eggs. Egg boxes hold 6 eggs each. How many egg boxes will she need?

2. Bags each hold 8 apples. George has picked 676 apples. How many bags will he fill?

3. For the school sports day, there are 369 children in teams of 7. How many teams will there be? How many children will be left over?

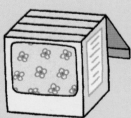

4. Julie needs 218 tiles for her bathroom. They are sold in boxes of 4. How many boxes does she need?

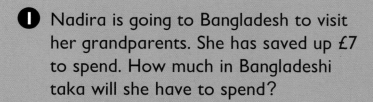

'Swap it Quick' Money Exchange

Today for £1 you will get:

```
  83  Bangladeshi taka
12.1  Danish kroner
 1.6  US dollars
   9  South African rand
   3  Cypriot pounds
 6.4  Polish zloties
 176  Japanese yen
```

1 Nadira is going to Bangladesh to visit her grandparents. She has saved up £7 to spend. How much in Bangladeshi taka will she have to spend?

2 Nadira's brother Kamul has £13. What amount of Bangladeshi taka will he have?

3 Jo has 78 Cypriot pounds left from her trip to Cyprus. How much will she have when she changes it back to UK pounds?

4 Charlie lives in South Africa. His aunt sends him £35 for his birthday. How much in rand will he have when he exchanges this?

5 Debbie is going to Denmark to visit a friend. Her mum has promised her £30 spending money. How much will she have in Danish kroner?

6 A box of chocolates at the airport costs £4. How much would you have to pay in US dollars?

7 A CD player costs 128 zloties in Poland. How much is that in UK pounds?

A

1 Ms Capaldi buys 16 bottles of orange juice for the school fair. Each bottle costs 35 pence. How much do they cost altogether?

2 Watermelons cost £1.92 for 6. How much does one cost?

3 Big bags of sweets cost £3.50. How much does she pay for 20?

4 Inside each big bag of sweets, there are 10 small bags. How much does each of these small bags cost?

5 She buys 9 boxes of chocolates for prizes. They cost £2.34 each. How much do the chocolates cost altogether?

B

1 Hiring a bouncy castle costs £9.45 altogether for the first three hours, then £2.50 for each extra hour. The fair lasts for 6 hours. How much will the hire cost be?

2 Jo is in charge of the bouncy castle and charges infants 5 pence and juniors 25 pence for each go. She takes £17.20. She knows 50 juniors had a go. How many infants went on the bouncy castle?

3 A crate of cola costs £4.53. Mr Long buys 7 crates. Ms Capaldi buys 2 more crates. How much do they spend altogether on cola for the drinks stall?

4 A crate holds 24 bottles. The drinks stall has 312 bottles of cola and lemonade altogether. How many crates of lemonade were bought for the drinks stall?

5 Bottles of cola cost 40 pence and bottles of lemonade cost 30 pence. If they sell all the bottles, how much money is taken?

6 Big boxes of crisps hold 16 packets each. There are 18 boxes of cheese and onion crisps and 24 boxes of plain crisps. How many packets are there in total?

16c

1 13 ? 8 ? 2 = 130
2 15 ? 3 ? 2 = 90
3 21 ? 7 ? 4 = 7

4 6 ? 14 ? 8 = 160
5 42 ? 6 ? 3 = 10
6 21 ? 4 ? 4 = 80

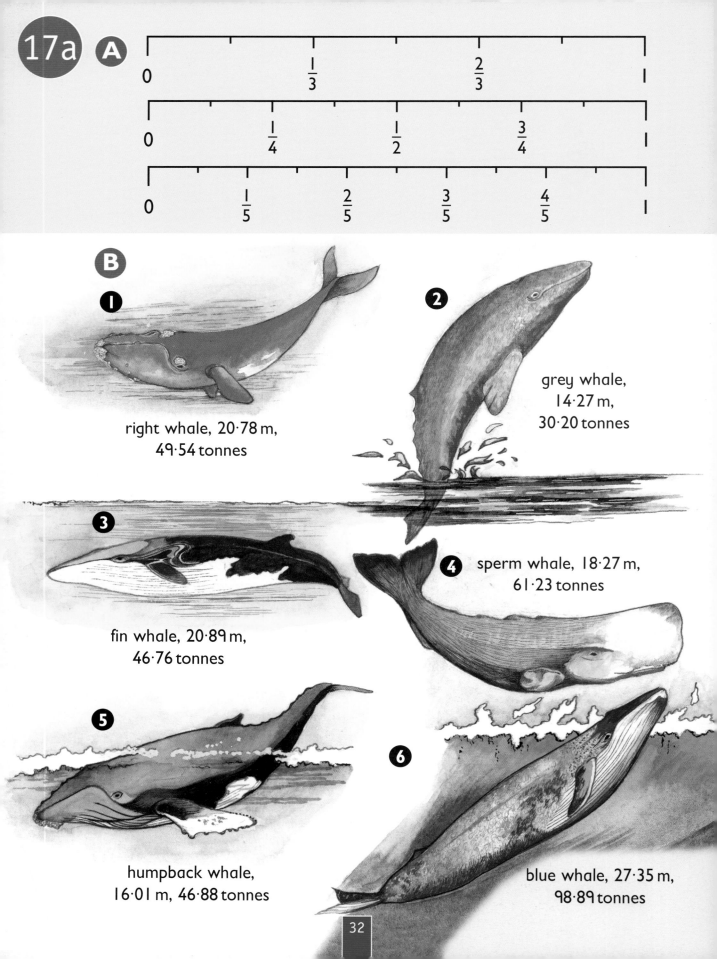

17a

A

(number lines showing fractions with thirds, quarters, and fifths)

0   1/3   2/3

0   1/4   1/2   3/4

0   1/5   2/5   3/5   4/5

B

1 right whale, 20·78 m, 49·54 tonnes

2 grey whale, 14·27 m, 30·20 tonnes

3 fin whale, 20·89 m, 46·76 tonnes

4 sperm whale, 18·27 m, 61·23 tonnes

5 humpback whale, 16·01 m, 46·88 tonnes

6 blue whale, 27·35 m, 98·89 tonnes

1

Julie has 12 sweets. She eats two thirds of them. How many sweets does she eat?

2

Harriet has a bag of 20 oranges. She puts three tenths of them in a bowl. How many does she put in the bowl?

3

Joe bakes 15 tarts. He puts four fifths of them in a box. How many does he put in the box?

4

Sam has 24 tennis balls. He takes three eighths of them out of the box to play a game. How many does he take out of the box?

5

Becky has an 80 cm length of ribbon. She cuts seven tenths of it off to make a hair band. What is the length of the hair band?

❶ ❷

❸ ❹

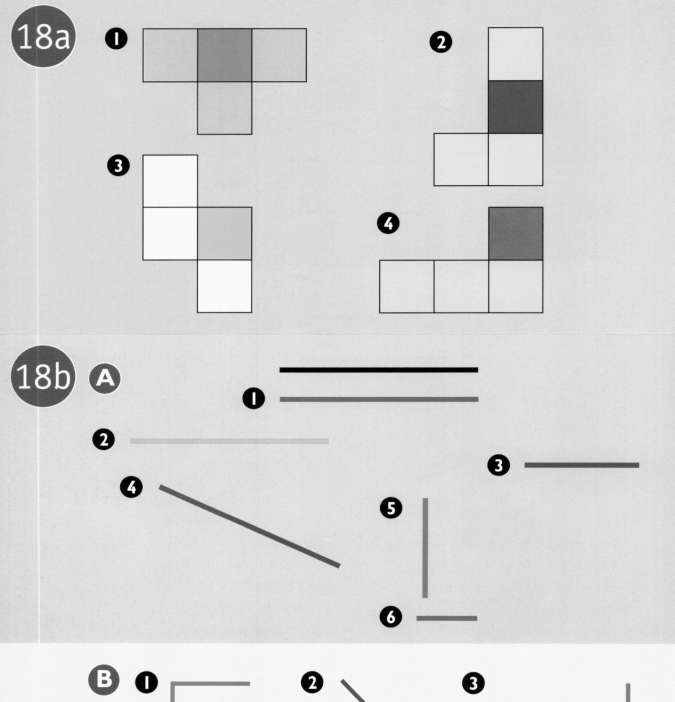

Ⓐ

❶

❷

❸

❹

❺

❻

Ⓑ ❶ ❷ ❸

❹ ❺ ❻

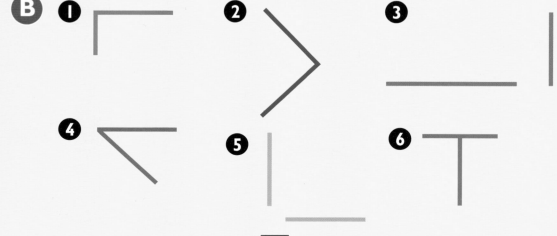

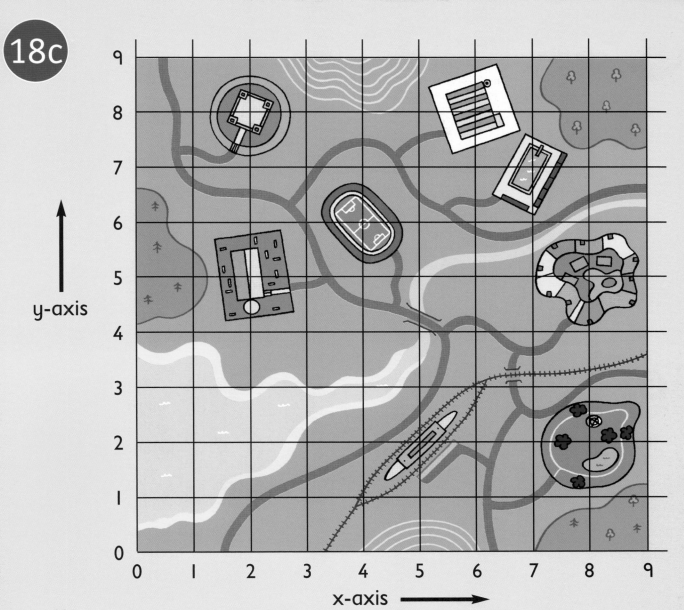

18c

y-axis →

x-axis →

Key

 Church

 Castle

 Factory

 Football pitch

 Park

 Swimming pool

 Train station

 Zoo

x	y	coordinate	object
2	5	(2, 5)	Church
4	6		
8	5		
5	2		
6	8		
7	7		
8	2		
2	8		

A

B

Angle 1 is larger than angle 2 because the arrow is longer.

Angle 1 and angle 2 are the same size because the amount of turn is the same.

Angle 2 is larger than angle 1 because the lines are longer.

A

1 **2** **3**

4

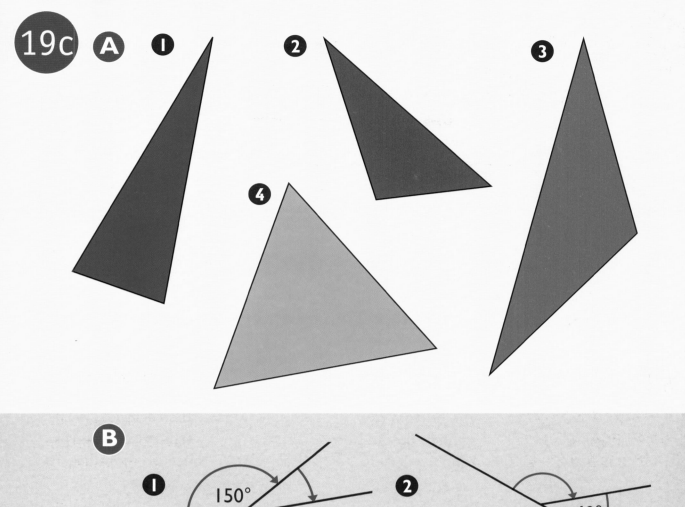

B

1 150°

2 40°

3 125°

4 25°

5 170°

6 35°

7 90°

8 15°

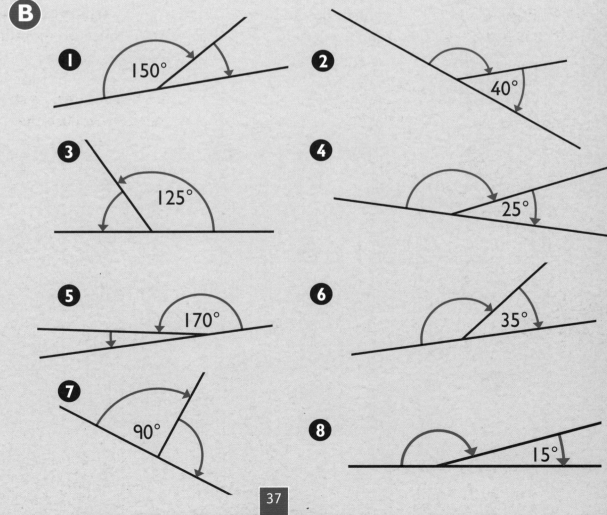

A

6 cm

5 cm 5 cm

6 cm

The area of the rectangle is 24 square centimetres because there are 6 squares in the bottom row, there are 4 squares above this row, and 6 x 4 is 24.

The area of the rectangle is 22 square centimetres because 6 plus 5 plus 6 plus 5 is 22.

The area of the rectangle is 30 square centimetres because there are 6 squares in the bottom row, 5 squares up the side and 6 x 5 is 30.

The area of the rectangle is 10 square centimetres because there are 10 squares on the picture.

B

1 6 cm x 4 cm

2 8 cm x 7 cm

3 11 cm x 5 cm

4 9 cm x 9 cm

5 10 cm x 12 cm

6 20 cm x 8 cm

7 22 cm x 13 cm

8 30 cm x 15 cm

20b

750 g	$\frac{1}{100}$ kg	$\frac{1}{2}$ kg	0·1 kg	10 g	$\frac{3}{4}$ kg
1·0 kg	500 g	0·75 kg	0·01 kg	0·25 kg	$\frac{1}{4}$ kg
$\frac{1}{10}$ kg	250 g	1 kg	1000 g	100 g	0·5 kg

20c

1. The zoomobile carries 65 kg. Could all the animals be transported together on 1 July?

2. On 1 March, how much heavier was the deer than the polar bear?

3. The zookeeper took the goat in the zoomobile at the beginning of November. She also took food for the monkeys. What mass of food could she take?
   There are nine monkeys. How much food did each one get?

4. In August, the polar bear ate 6·8 kg of fish per day. How much did it eat in 7 days?

5. On 1 November, how much heavier was the polar bear than the deer?

21a

1. Gordon is driving a coach-load of tourists from Athens to Amsterdam. He drives 2808 km, and then has a puncture 209 km away from Athens. How far is Athens from Amsterdam?

2. The Go Girl! band is becoming more popular. At Linacre Stadium they had an audience of 6981 in March, and 7011 in April. How many more people came in April?

3. Farmer Sprout bought a brand-new combine harvester for £8007. She paid £105 as a deposit. How much more does she have left to pay?

4. Captain Nimmo's submarine descended to 6005 metres in the sea. It then rose by 19 metres. What depth did it rise to?

Mini football and goal set £4.72

Street hockey training set £9.53

Hockey balls 87p each

Two bats and a softball £5.78

Plastic football £3.47

Softballs 34p each

Golf balls 66p each

Swingball set with bats £14.29

Golf set £11.66

Yoyo £1.39

Kangaroo hopper £3.55

Netball stand and ball £15.75

21c Ⓐ 134   87   221   376   510   355   268

Ⓑ

Calculation	Display	Correct answer	Check
4578 − 986	3682	3592	3592 + 986 = 4578
4652 − 865	3787		
2567 + 395	2567395		
528 + 6539	7067		
1489 + 567	844263		
8305 − 2187	6118		
7069 + 388	7107		
4555 − 768	44787		
483 + 5809	6292		

1

Name: Ronnie	Number of lengths: 9
Sponsor	amount per length
dad	42p
mum	55p
sister	4p
gran	£1.20

2

Name: Janine	Number of lengths: 14
Sponsor	amount per length
mum	70p
brother	26p
uncle	£1.99
dog	15p

3

Name: Majid	Number of lengths: 7
Sponsor	amount per length
brother	35p
sister	30p
sister	11p

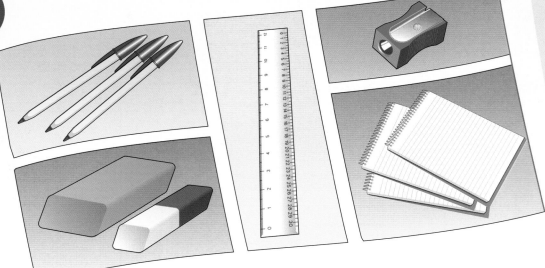

12 pens   99p per box

15 erasers   18p per box

5 sharpeners   £1.04 per box

10 notepads   89p per box

25 rulers   £3.98 per box

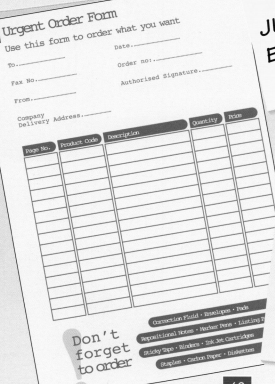

Urgent Order Form
Use this form to order what you want

To:...........................

Fax No:...........................

From:...........................

Company
Delivery Address:...........................

Date:...........................

Order no:...........................

Authorised Signature:...........................

Page No.	Product Code	Description	Quantity	Price

Don't
forget
to order

Correction Fluid · Envelopes · Pads
Repositional Notes · Marker Pens · Listing P
Sticky Tape · Binders · Ink Jet Cartridges
Staples · Carbon Paper · Diskettes

JUST GET ME 3 OF EVERY BOX.
          MRS GRUMP

I need 5 of every box because we missed out last time.
          Miss Dout

I've got 30 kids and they need one of everything. You decide how many I need.
          Mr Errwell

22c

1 A dog chased 14 cats and twice as many squirrels up into a tree. How many animals are hiding in the tree?

2

Agnes gave her 4 grandchildren £27 each for Christmas. She spent £123 on the rest of the family. How much did she spend altogether?

3

Soraya reads for 45 minutes every school day. She reads for twice as long each night at the weekend. For how long does she read each week?

4

Jumi has spent £27 on shoes, £1.99 on a magazine and £3.77 on a snack. She had £2.23 left in her purse. How much did she start with?

5 School dinners cost £1.27 each. Michael needs to pay for 9 days' school dinners. How much dinner money does he need?

6 Carlton buys six 1·2 kg boxes of strawberries and two 3·5 kg boxes. What weight of strawberries does he buy altogether?

7 Nellie buys her favourite chocolate bar every day. It costs her £2.73 each week. How much does each bar cost?

1

0	0	1	2	3
4	4	5	6	7
8	8	9	10	11
12	12	13	14	15
16	16	17	18	19

2

0	0	1	2	3
4	5	6	7	8

3

0	1	2	3	4
5	6	7	8	9

4

0	0	1	2	2
3	4	4	5	6
7	7	8	9	9
10	11	11	12	13

A

1 multiples of 2 and multiples of 5
2 multiples of 3 and multiples of 5
3 multiples of 6 and multiples of 2
4 multiples of 9 and multiples of 2
5 multiples of 2 and multiples of 7
6 multiples of 2 and multiples of 11
7 multiples of 3 and multiples of 10
8 multiples of 4 and multiples of 5

B

| 10 | 5 | 4 | 100 | 2 |

1
700 600
200 1200
1600   400
500

2
12   768
44   536   50
214   348
156   70
92

3
216   520
724 228 932
136   340
144   548
252

4
125   85
60   195
320   55
715   355

5
50   60
790 80 40
330   70 120
260

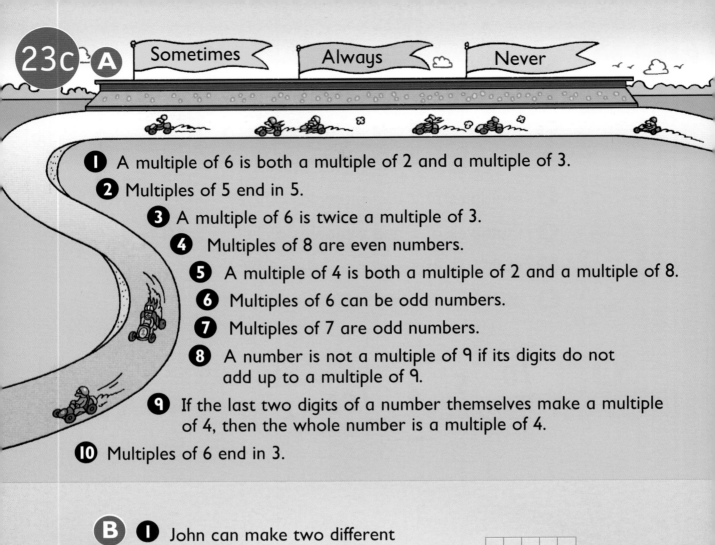

A

Sometimes   Always   Never

1. A multiple of 6 is both a multiple of 2 and a multiple of 3.

2. Multiples of 5 end in 5.

3. A multiple of 6 is twice a multiple of 3.

4. Multiples of 8 are even numbers.

5. A multiple of 4 is both a multiple of 2 and a multiple of 8.

6. Multiples of 6 can be odd numbers.

7. Multiples of 7 are odd numbers.

8. A number is not a multiple of 9 if its digits do not add up to a multiple of 9.

9. If the last two digits of a number themselves make a multiple of 4, then the whole number is a multiple of 4.

10. Multiples of 6 end in 3.

B

1. John can make two different rectangles from the number 15.

Can you find a number that makes exactly four different rectangles?

2. Jo sets the constant function on her calculator to add the same number each time, starting from a single-digit number. Part of the sequence goes like this:

... 45   53   61   69   77   ...

What was the single-digit starting number?

3. Sam makes a repeating pattern with these counters:

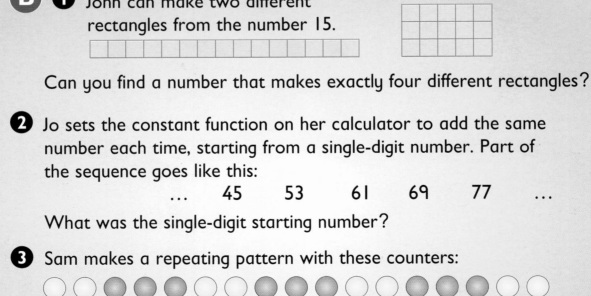

What colour will the thirty-seventh counter be?
What position in the line is the fourteenth blue counter?

1. $3876 + 5004 = \square$
2. $39 \times 40 = \square$
3. $19 \times 13 = \square$
4. $6 \cdot 2 - 2 \cdot 5 = \square$
5. $800 \times 5 = \square$
6. $28 \times \square = 140$
7. $6 \cdot 2 + \square = 8$
8. $853 - \square = 543$
9. $\square \div 2 = 176$
10. $7400 \div \square = 74$

24b

In my pocket I have:
one 20p coin
one 10p coin
one 5p coin
one 2p coin
one 1p coin

1. I pull out two coins.
   What different amounts can I make?

2. I pull out three coins.
   What different amounts can I make?

3. I pull out four coins.
   What different amounts can I make?

4. What amounts can't I make?
   Why not?

1

38 600   39 000

2

0   1000

3
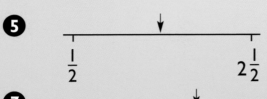
−7   −4

4

−10 °C   40 °C

5

$\frac{1}{2}$ $2\frac{1}{2}$

6

9:30   12:30

7
3 kg   4 kg

8
130 cm   140 cm

B

ENGLAND WIN ASHES

How to Cheat at Maths

2 + 2 = 5

A

① 9753 ② 6395 ③ 3876

④ 8547 ⑤ 5735 ⑥ 4865

⑦ 6841 ⑧ 4251 ⑨ 5732

B

①
For EEZEE Airlines to Barcelona is a flea hop!

Barcelona is 1547 km from London.

②
We even deliver to HIGH POINT FLATS! is no distance to our team!

High Point Flats are 882 m from Mega Superstore.

③
Large _____ bag of DOG NIBBLETS down in PRICE!

A large bag of Dog Nibblets weighs 5126 grams.

④
Our TAXIS will get you to the GRAND HOTEL in _____ !

The taxi journey from Main Station to the Grand Hotel was 12 minutes 25 seconds.

⑤
TEA IN NO TIME! The WHIZZO boils a litre of water within _____ !

The Whizzo Kettle boils a litre of water in 2 minutes 48 seconds.

⑥
So Small it fits into a space just _____ wide!

The Compact Computer Table is 132 cm wide.

① 36 ÷ 5   **②** 47 ÷ 2   **③** 25 ÷ 6

④ 54 ÷ 7   **⑤** 38 ÷ 9   **⑥** 77 ÷ 4

⑦ 56 ÷ 10   **⑧** 19 ÷ 4   **⑨** 49 ÷ 5

⑩ 45 ÷ 4

26b

① I have 330 chocolates.
A box holds 24 chocolates.
How many boxes can I fill?

② How many boxes
do I need to store
the chocolates?

④ Six friends went ice-skating.
The total cost was £15.60.
How much did each person
have to pay?

③ Twelve children can sit around a
table. There are 403 children in a
school. How many tables are needed
for the whole school to sit down?

⑤ A computer game costs
£29. How many games
can I buy with £190?

⑥ I save £3 every week. How many
weeks will it take me to save up for
a cycle helmet costing £39.90?

26c

1. $4000 \div 40$
2. $348 \div 3$
3. $630 \div 2$
4. $417 \div 7$
5. $344 \div 8$
6. $150 \div 6$

27a

1

×	300	600	
40	12 000		
20			18 000
10			

2

×	10	20	
300			9000
600		12 000	
900			

3

×	300	50	
20			
500			45 000
400			

4

×		70	
	4000		
800	64 000		
		49 000	63 000

51

27b

1 43×27

	40	3
20	$40 \times 20 = 800$	$3 \times 20 = 60$
7	$40 \times 7 = 280$	$3 \times 7 = 21$

$43 \times 27 = 800 + 280 + 60 + 21 = 1161$

2 24×32

	20	4
30		
2		

3 57×25

20		
5		

4 68×73

5 83×94

27c

A
1. 54×36
2. 42×35
3. 62×23
4. 54×72
5. 67×93

B
1. 54×36
2. 44×53
3. 26×61
4. 74×52
5. 91×83

1

Chow 2·5kg

Woof-woof 1750g

2

COLA 1·5 l

LEMONADE 2000 ml

3

Peanut butter 0·5kg

Choc spread 450g

4

450 ml

0·5 l

5

95 cm   1·5 m

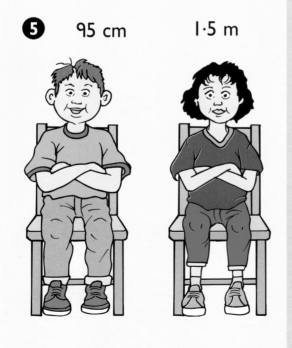

6

LOCH NESS
230 m deep

LAKE BAIKAL
1·7 km DEEP

1

A piece of dress material is 1·5 metres long. Sara cuts off a piece one third of this length.

How long is the piece left over?

2 A packet of cat food weighs 1·5 kilograms. The cat has eaten two fifths of the packet.

How many grams of the cat food has the cat eaten?

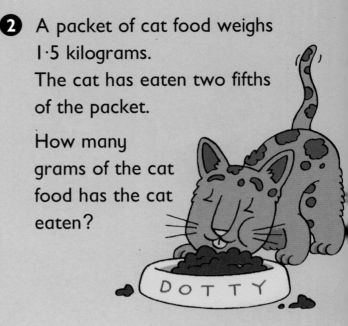

3

A tin of dog food weighs 1·2 kilograms. The dog eats two thirds of the tin of food.

How many grams of the food has the dog eaten?

4 A full bottle of lemonade holds 1·5 litres. Seven tenths of the lemonade has been drunk.

How many millilitres have been drunk?

5

The price of a television is normally £255.75. In a sale, two fifths of the price is taken off.

What is the price of the television in the sale?

1

At a tennis club there is 1 boy for every 3 girls. There are 10 boys at the club. How many girls are there?

2

Beverley and Joe get pocket money. Because she is younger, Beverley gets 2p for every 5p that Joe gets. Joe gets 50p pocket money. How much does Beverley get?

3

To get to work in a factory, 3 people use the train for every 5 people that use the bus. There are 60 people who use the train. How many people use the bus?

4

In a traffic survey at Southgate Road school, for every 2 lorries that go past there are 7 cars. In one hour, 20 lorries go past. How many cars go past?

5

Sharif's mum says she will give him £5 for every £4 pounds he saves himself. Sharif saves £24. How much money should his mum give him?

6

Courtney has a bunch of grapes. For every 3 grapes she eats she gives 4 grapes to her friends. She gives 16 grapes to her friends. How many grapes does she eat herself?

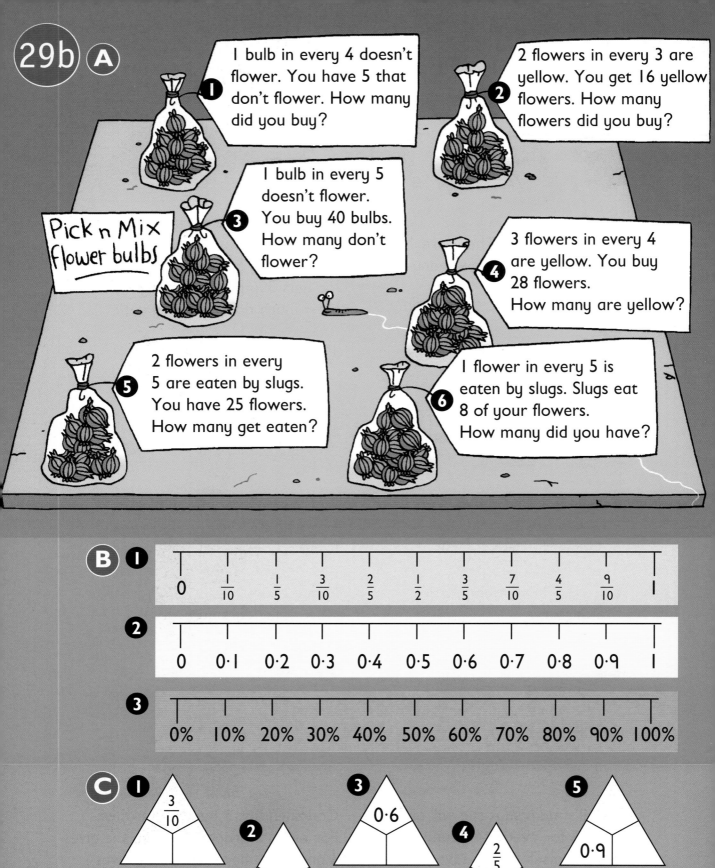

Keyboard £400
30% OFF

Game console £100
20% OFF

Electric guitar
£190
10% OFF

Video camera £800
60% OFF

Instant camera £6
10% OFF

Binoculars
£200
25% OFF

Mini system £150
40% OFF

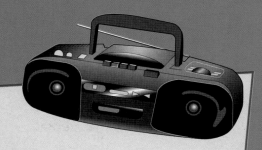

Radio/Cassette recorder £50
50% OFF

1 The City Farm is making a square paddock for the horses, the cows and the sheep. The perimeter of the square is 286 metres. What length of fencing is needed along each side of the paddock?

2 Woolly the sheep is 96 cm high. Black Star the horse is 148 cm high. Buttercup the cow is halfway between Woolly and Black Star. How high is Buttercup?

3 The least and greatest heights of the animals in the City Farm paddock are 47·3 cm and 153·7 cm. What is the range of the heights of the animals in the paddock?

4 Black Star the horse drank 10·5 l of water yesterday. Woolly the sheep drank 4·16 l of water. How much more did Black Star drink than Woolly?

5 Each rabbit in the City Farm eats 45 grams of pellets a day. There are 23 rabbits. How long will a 30 kg bag of pellets last?

Calculation	Key sequence	Display	Correct answer
15 × 15	`1` `5` `+` `1` `5` `=`	30	225
465 − 365	`4` `6` `5` `−` `3` `6` `5` `=` `=`	− 265	
256 + 312	`2` `5` `6` `3` `1` `2`	256312	
26 × 53	`2` `6` `+` `5` `3` `=`	79	
4 + (5 × 20)	`4` `+` `5` `×` `2` `0` `=`	180	
112 × 234	`1` `1` `2` `×` `3` `2` `4` `=`	36288	
627 ÷ 19	`6` `2` `7` `×` `1` `9` `=`	11913	
627 ÷ 19	`6` `2` `7` `−` `1` `9` `=`	608	
627 ÷ 19	`6` `2` `7` `÷` `1` `9` `=` `=`	1·7368421	
8 − (105 ÷ 21)	`8` `+` `1` `0` `5` `÷` `2` `1`	5·3809523	

❶
Pizza £5.76
Cola £0.95
Choc 74p
£2.07 for salad
Ice 82p

Total

❷
Burger £3.99
Chips 64p
Egg £0.56
Banana split 153p
Tea 25p

Total

❸
Lasagne 455p
Tomatoes £0.92
Bread 22p
Fudge cake £1.05
Squash 38p

Total

❹
Steak £9.34
Mash 342p
Peas £0.95
Trifle 487p
Coffee 85p

Total

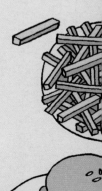

B

The bill	Shared between	Amount to pay each
£3.56	4 friends	
£2.60	5 friends	
£1.84		92p
£24.18	6 friends	
	3 friends	£1.82
£12.00		40p
	8 friends	£1.30
£11.22		£1.02

C

1 Wanda the waitress sells large slices of pizza to take away at £3.40 each. On Tuesday she sells 18 slices. How much money does she collect?

2 On Wednesday, Walter the waiter collects £71.40. How many large slices of pizza does he sell?

3 For the last hour of the day pizza slices are sold at 25% off the price. Callam buys 6 slices. How much does he save?

4 You can get 12 slices from an enormous pizza. Lisa buys two and a half pizzas. What does this cost her?

5 If you buy 6 pizzas you get a 50% discount. How much is the discount?

Pizza
£3.40 per slice

①

Number of children at Halley Court School entering the mini-marathon

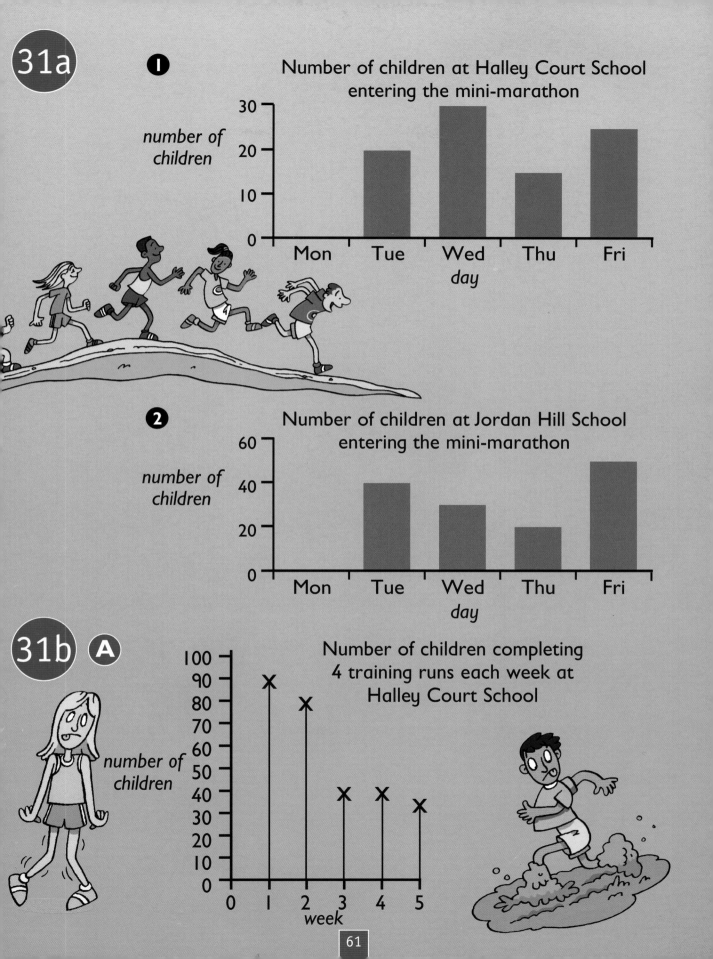

number of children

②

Number of children at Jordan Hill School entering the mini-marathon

number of children

A

Number of children completing 4 training runs each week at Halley Court School

number of children

Children completing 4 training runs at Jordan Hill School

Week	1	2	3	4	5
Number of children	140	65	70	30	35

31c

Record of training runs

	James	Andrea	Eric	Alex	Neelam
100 metres	//	0	/	//	///
400 metres	0	/	0	0	0
800 metres	/	/	/	0	//
1 kilometre	0	//	/	0	/

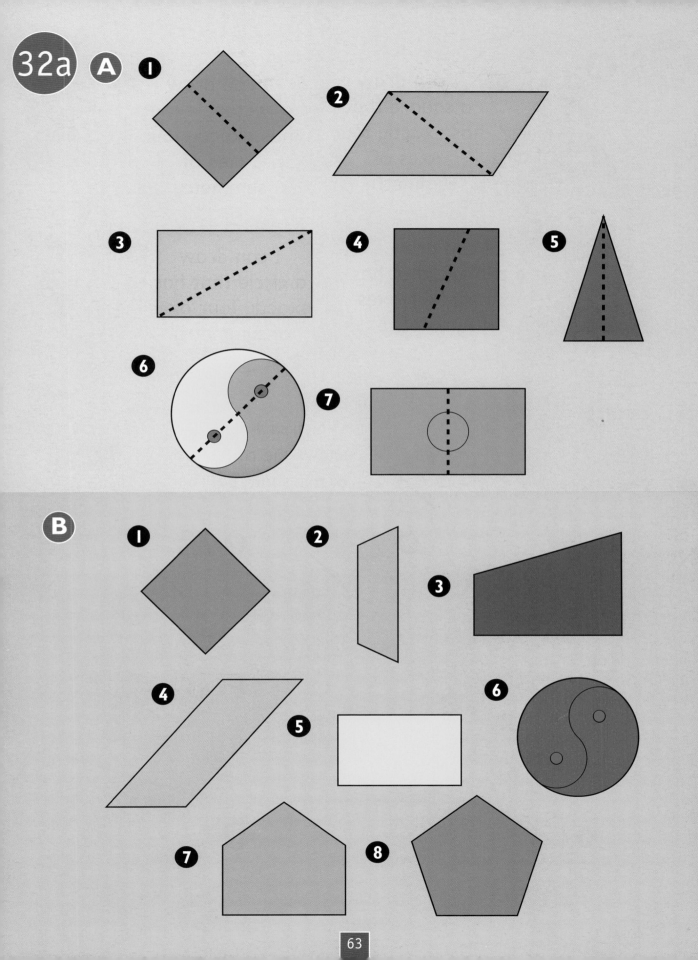

32a

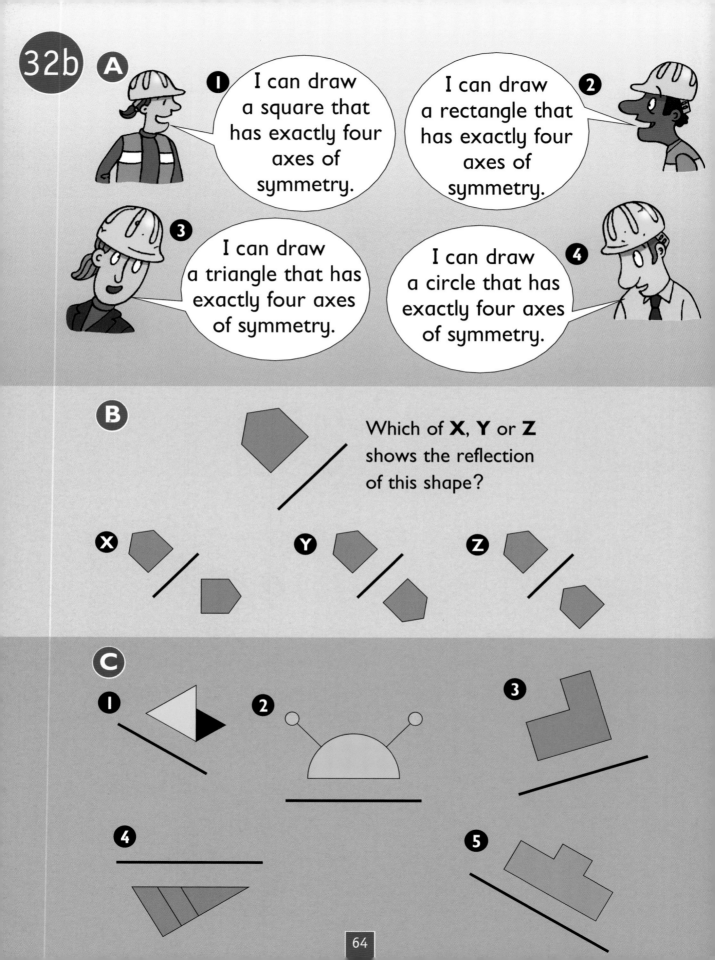

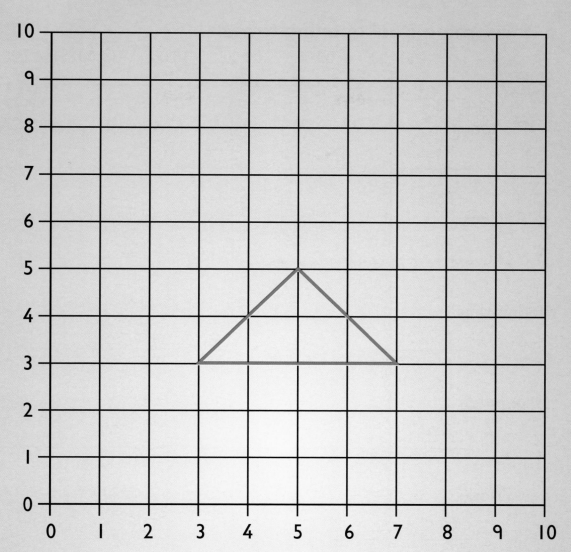

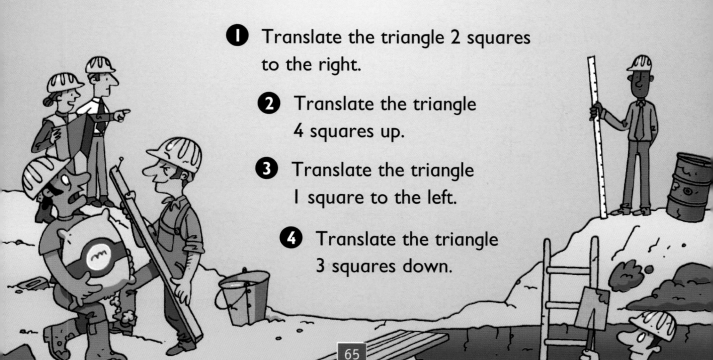

1 Translate the triangle 2 squares to the right.

2 Translate the triangle 4 squares up.

3 Translate the triangle 1 square to the left.

4 Translate the triangle 3 squares down.

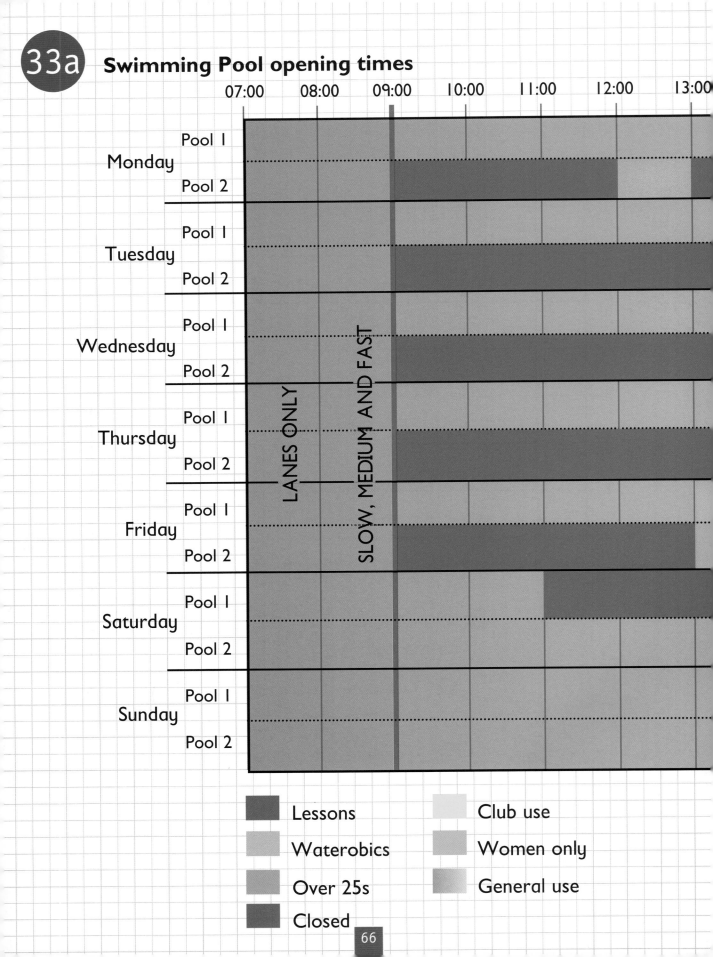

33a Swimming Pool opening times

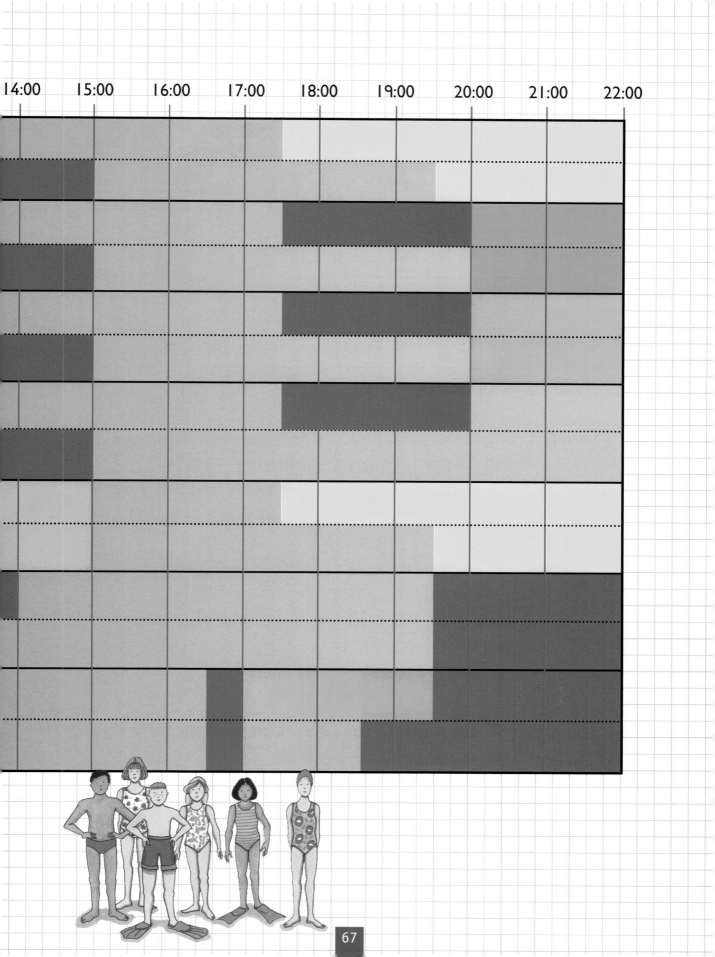

A

London						
211	Aberystwyth					
115	125	Bristol				
57	154	72	Oxford			
397	319	366	356	Glasgow		
185	138	161	144	215	Manchester	
160	175	164	135	247	38	Sheffield

(distances in miles)

B **1** A lorry driver drives back and forth between London and Oxford 6 times in a day. How many miles does he drive?

2 How much further is Glasgow than Bristol from London?

3 Driving at 60 miles an hour, approximately how many hours will it take to drive from London to Aberystwyth?

4 If you went from Glasgow to Sheffield then on to Oxford in a day, how many miles would you have travelled?

5 Is it true to say that Glasgow is more than twice as far from London than Manchester is?

6 Which cities are about 400 miles apart?

 **C**

From London to	Average journey time by train
Aberystwyth	5 hours
Bristol	1 hour 20 minutes
Oxford	50 minutes
Glasgow	5 hours 45 minutes
Manchester	3 hours
Sheffield	2 hours 20 minutes

1 If Jane left London by car at 10:00, and Kate caught the 11:25 train from London St Pancras, who is likely to arrive in Sheffield first?

2 If Murray left London by car at 14:15 and Toby caught the 14:15 train from London Paddington, who is likely to arrive in Bristol first?

3 Thea is travelling by car to Aberystwyth. Ffion is travelling by train to Manchester. If they both leave London at 18:00, who will arrive at their destination first?

4 Liz leaves London on the 17:25 train for Manchester. There is a 40-minute delay en-route. If Ashia left Glasgow at 16:00 by car, about how long is she waiting at the station for Liz in Manchester?

5 Allowing for short delays, would I arrive in better time for a 19:30 concert in Oxford if I left London by rail at 17:50 or by car at 18:00?

6 Rosemary and Fatima want to meet and spend a day in Oxford. Rosemary is travelling by car from Aberystwyth and Fatima is travelling by car from Bristol. If they are meeting at 11:00, what is the latest they should each leave home?

34a

CHOKE
66p a litre

FUME
70p a litre

MONOX
80p a litre

SLICK
60p a litre

GASSO
64p a litre

SMOG
75p a litre

Marvin's Marvellous Medicines

Teacher Tickle

0·35 l spinach juice

750 ml cod liver oil

0·05 l slug juice

0·15 l crushed nettles

Hairy Happener

250 ml tooth whitener

0·150 l crushed nettles

20 ml chilli sauce

0·1 l spinach juice

Halloween Hizz

0·35 l slug juice

0·4 l crushed nettles

55 ml tooth whitener

Weekend Whizzer

0·55 l spinach juice

600 ml chilli sauce

45 ml tooth whitener

Dinosaur Drops

175 ml tooth whitener

250 ml cod liver oil

15 ml chilli sauce

1 Chloe, who is 4 years old, is poorly. She has to be given two 5 ml spoonfuls of medicine 3 times per day. If the doctor tells her mother, who is a teacher, to do this for 7 days and the medicine bottle contains 250 ml, how much will be left at the end of the treatment?

2 Dot is holding her annual bonfire party. She wants to make tomato soup. If each large white polystyrene cup holds 200 ml and she expects 50 guests aged between 1 and 99, approximately how much soup should she make so that everyone has a cup?

3 Sally fills her watering can, which cost £6.50, and holds 5 litres. It has a hole in it and is leaking. If she has 2850 ml left when she finds the hole, how much water has Sally lost?

4 To fill up our car, which is blue, we need 8 gallons. If petrol from the Tiger service station on the corner is 70p per litre, how much roughly will it cost us?

5 To get the correct shade of purple, Tyrone mixes 500 ml of blue paint for every 750 ml of red paint. If his final mixture contains 2·5 l of blue paint, how much purple paint does he have altogether?

6 Murray, who is 39 years old, has a van that is always dirty. It does 10 miles to the litre. How many litres will it use up on a 140 mile journey if we are going west out of London?

7 When the plug is pulled out of the Dale family's bath, water drains away at 1 pint every 6 seconds. If the bath has bubble bath in and it is a Tuesday, about how long will it take to drain away 90 litres?

8 The Edge family, who have 4 children and 2 cats, order 6 pints of milk per day every day except Sunday. If Mrs Edge decides to buy it from the supermarket instead, which is 2 kilometres away, how many 4-litre plastic bottles will she need for a week?

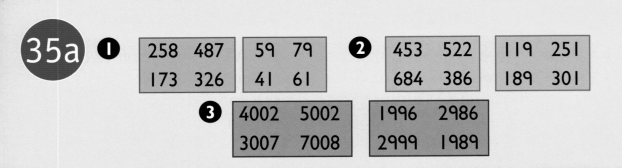

35a

1

258	487
173	326

59	79
41	61

2

453	522
684	386

119	251
189	301

3

4002	5002
3007	7008

1996	2986
2999	1989

35b

A   16·7   8·4   7·9   25·1   17·2   25·6   8·8

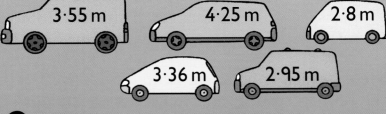

B

1 Grange School has a parking area 18 metres long, and just one vehicle wide. Can these five cars and vans fit in the car park?

3·55 m   4·25 m   2·8 m   3·36 m   2·95 m

2 Mr Hill has a car with a trailer, measuring 9·24 m. The trailer is 4·78 m. How long is the car?

3 The cable car will take a maximum weight of 350 kg. Should 5 people weighing 55·2 kg, 56·7 kg, 80·4 kg, 74·8 kg and 92·3 kg get into the cable car together?

4 Four people weighing 253·1 kg get on the cable car. A small child weighing 27·6 kg gets off. What is the total weight of the passengers now?

5 Kisi went to the DIY shop to buy the paint and tools below. He took £25 with him. Was this enough?

£5.82   £4.95   £3.37   £6.25   £4.43

6 Kisi spent £8.57 on a hammer and a set of nails. The set of nails was the wrong size, so Kisi got his money back. He spent £5.78 on the hammer. How much were the nails?

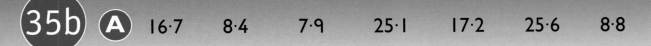

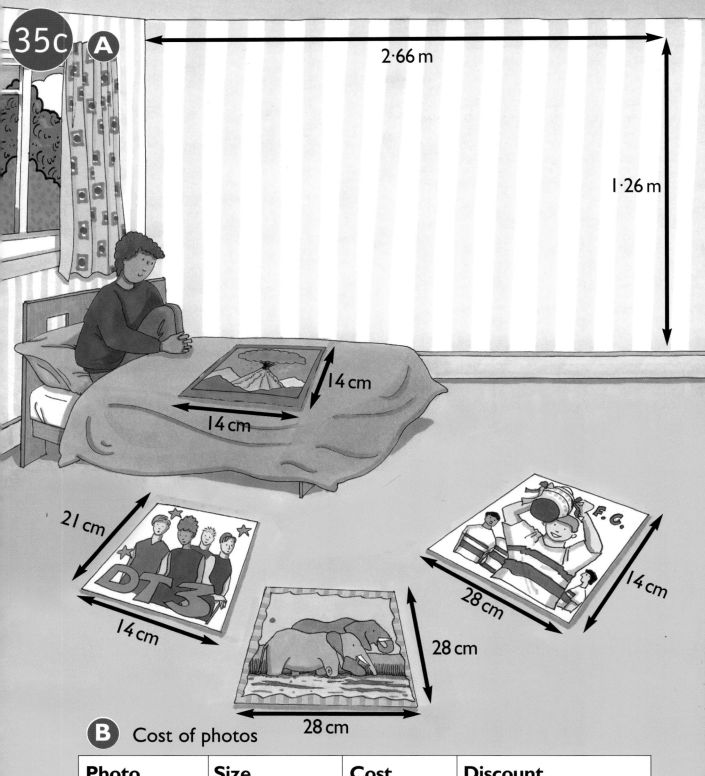

A

2·66 m

1·26 m

14 cm

14 cm

21 cm

14 cm

28 cm

28 cm

28 cm

14 cm

B Cost of photos

Photo	Size	Cost	Discount
Pop groups	14 cm x 21 cm	2 for £2.50	50% if you buy 20
Animals	28 cm x 28 cm	£1.24 each	Buy 10, get 25% off
Football teams	28 cm x 14 cm	£2. 65 each	6 for the price of 5
Volcanoes	14 cm x 14 cm	4 for £2	Buy 16 and get 1 free

36a **A**

1. 4
2. 18
3. 28
4. 63
5. 80
6. 99
7. 72
8. 36
9. 84
10. 105

B
1. 24 × 12
2. 18 × 15
3. 12 × 28
4. 21 × 16
5. 33 × 9
6. 14 × 15
7. 32 × 13
8. 15 × 16

True or false?

1 1938 + 5744 = 7681

2 5223 + 6851 = 12 074

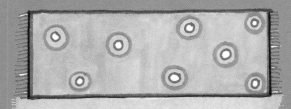

3 9874 − 6531 = 3343

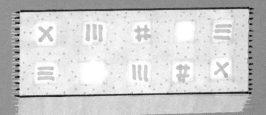

4 762 + 684 + 392 = 1837

5 6421 − 4847 = 1573

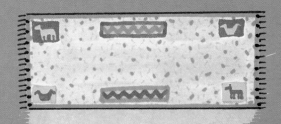

6 6245 + 7912 = 14 157

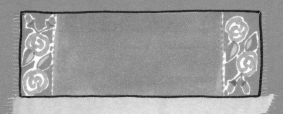

7 585 + 647 + 151 = 1378

8 332 + 695 + 157 = 1184

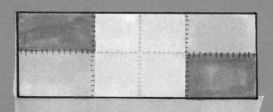

9 1352 − 1278 = 74

10 4221 − 1758 = 2464